SAFE AT HOME

Robert Skead, Safe at Home

ISBN 978-0-9821652-1-8

Cross Training Publishing
PO Box 1874
Kearney, NE 68848
(308) 293-3891

This book is manufactured in the United States of America.

Library of Congress Cataloging in Publication Data in Progress.

Published by Cross Training Publishing,
PO Box 1874
Kearney, NE 68848
Website: crosstrainingpublishing.com

For my son Trevor,
who reached Home before I did.
You will not return to me, but I will go to you.

"Every day is a new opportunity.
You can build on yesterday's success
or put its failures behind and start over again.
That's the way life is.
With a new game every day.
And that's the way baseball is."

Bob Feller
Indians Pitcher (1936-56)

CHAPTER ONE

Leading Off

"Fifty thousand dollars!" exclaimed eleven-year-old Trevor Mitchell. He couldn't believe it. He looked at his dad who was standing next to him looking dazed, his mouth wide open.

"That's what the book says," replied Charlie, the owner of Charlie's Sports Collectibles. "This is beautiful! Where did you get this?" Charlie asked Trevor and his father.

Trevor's father was still speechless. Hearing the words *fifty thousand dollars'* will do that to most people. "Say what?" Trevor's father said and shook himself out of his trance. "Oh, I'm sorry. It was my grandfather's card. He gave it to my son yesterday."

"Well, I'll be . . ." Charlie answered. He looked at the card as if it were a beautiful diamond. "A 1915 rookie Babe Ruth card . . . in mint condition. In all my years of collecting, I've never seen one in person. You say it was your grandfather's?"

"My *great*-grandfather's," Trevor replied, not knowing that Charlie was addressing his father.

"I thought it might be valuable, but I never imagined anything like this," said Trevor's dad. "That's why we're here. I didn't want Trevor to . . . well, you know. "

"First things first," Charlie said, taking out a sturdy plastic cardholder. "Let's make sure this baby stays protected." He slipped the card carefully into the holder with the precision of an expert.

"This is in perfect condition. Where has it been?" Charlie asked.

"My grandfather kept it in a special place in the back of his Bible."

"I see," said Charlie. "Mr. . . . .?"

"Mitchell," Trevor's dad filled in.

"Mr. Mitchell, this is a spectacular card. It may even be worth a little more than fifty thousand. This book is six months old."

"Wow," Trevor exclaimed, his blue eyes growing wider. He scratched his blonde head. Being young, Trevor didn't fully appreciate the value of the dollar, but he could tell from everyone's reaction that this card was special. Its dollar value meant little in comparison to the value it had because of who it came from and the amazing story behind it.

A man who was browsing through the shop came over to look at the card. His name was Mike Tripuka. Charlie knew Mike's profession, but Trevor and his dad had no idea who he was.

"May I?" Mike asked Trevor's father.

"Sure," he said handing him the card, now protected from harm in its new plastic case.

"Wow, Babe Ruth. The Sultan of Swat. He was an incredible hitter."

"The best," added Charlie.

"Not many people know, but 'The Babe' was also a great pitcher," Mike added.

Trevor's eyebrows rose with interest. He really wanted to say something, but his dad taught him not to interrupt adults while they were speaking.

"Babe Ruth himself said his favorite record is the one he held for twenty-nine and two thirds of consecutive scoreless innings pitched in World Series play."

"I know he was a great pitcher!" Trevor proclaimed.

All the men turned their attention to Trevor, impressed by his statement.

"My great-grandpa told me. My great-grandpa played baseball with Babe Ruth. That's why he has this card."

"How old is your great-grandfather?" Charlie asked.

"A century! Isn't that awesome?" Trevor answered.

"He turned one hundred yesterday," Trevor's father added.

"Well, I'll be," Charlie said shaking his head in wonder. "That is wonderful!"

"Really?" Mike replied with interest.

Charlie glanced up at him. He had an idea what Mike was thinking. That's because Mike Tripuka was the local sportswriter—and like all writers, he was always looking for a good story.

"One hundred years old?" Mike repeated. "And you say he played ball with Babe Ruth? In the majors?"

"Yep," Trevor said proudly.

His dad guessed what was coming next, and started to feel a bit awkward.

"My great-grandpa even stole home while 'The Babe' was pitching. He was the only person to ever do it."

The store fell silent for a moment as they each digested what Trevor said. Mike and Charlie weren't quite sure if this was true or just the made-up story of an imaginative child.

They looked at Trevor's dad who was still feeling awkward because he knew how unbelievable the statement sounded. He paused for a second and then said, "It's true."

Mike Tripuka had to think fast. A one-hundred-year-old man who played ball with Babe Ruth. He even stole home while "The Babe" was pitching. A fifty thousand dollar card. Then his mouth started to move before he even realized what he was about to say. "May I talk to your grandfather sometime?" he asked Mr. Mitchell. "I'm Mike Tripuka, sportswriter for the *Suburban Times*. I'd really like to meet him."

Trevor's dad hesitated for a moment. He looked into Mike's eyes, knowing that a person's eyes revealed a great deal about who they are. He knew how some reporters distorted the truth. He also knew that some reporters lied. But Mike looked right back at Mr. Mitchell without wavering. His eyes showed a natural warmth and sincerity.

"Sure," Mr. Mitchell replied, feeling that Mike was trustworthy. "I'll give you our number. He lives with us. Call me, and I'll see what I can do."

Charlie handed Mike a piece of paper. Mike gave the paper to Mr. Mitchell and pulled out a pen from his blazer. Mr. Mitchell wrote down a phone number and handed it back to Mike.

"Thanks," Mike said, extending his hand.

"No problem," Mr. Mitchell replied and they shook hands.

As he let go of his grip, Mr. Mitchell could not help but

wonder if he was doing the right thing. He knew his grandpa's story well–and he believed every word of it. But he couldn't help but wonder if he had just opened up a can of worms that should have remained closed. Since his own father had passed away three years earlier, Grandpa was still the honorary head of the family. His grandpa was the man who taught his father about what was important in life: God, family, honor and integrity. His father, in turn, taught him–and now he was trying to instill those same values in Trevor. One thing was certain. Mr. Mitchell would never do anything to intentionally hurt his grandfather.

Should I have given him our number? What would this reporter write? A story about a 100th birthday or a story about a crazy old man who says he stole home off Babe Ruth? Grandfather's story was deemed unbelievable by most people who heard it. *What have I done?* thought Trevor's dad.

"Well, thanks for the information," Mr. Mitchell told Charlie.

Charlie tried to hand the card to Trevor's dad.

"That card isn't mine. It belongs to my son."

Charlie smiled and returned the precious card to Trevor. "Take good care of that, Sport."

"I will," Trevor said solemnly.

Mr. Mitchell reached for his wallet. "How much do I owe for the case?" he asked.

"Nothing," Charlie said. "I should pay you for the privilege of seeing it–and holding it."

"I don't know about that."

"Hey, you guys made my day. That card is a thing of beauty," Charlie said.

"Thanks, that's really nice of you," Trevor's dad replied, putting his wallet away.

9

"If you ever wanna sell it . . . I can help!" Charlie added.

Trevor's father chuckled. "I don't think so. It's kind of a family heirloom. But thanks."

"I'll be in touch!" Mike Tripuka exclaimed, as Trevor and his dad made their way to the door.

"Bye!" yelled Trevor. "Thanks!"

Trevor looked up at his dad and smiled. His dad put his arm around him and opened the door.

The two men remaining in the shop looked at each other as if what had just transpired was something magical. As Trevor and his dad left the store, Trevor held the card tightly in his hand and pondered thoughts of his great-grandpa. The two shared a very special bond, and both of them loved and admired the game of baseball.

Little did Trevor know that the card he held in his hand would change his life.

CHAPTER TWO
Value Lesson

Trevor's dad leaned back against the kitchen counter. "I don't think we should let him keep it," he said, almost whispering.

"Why not?" asked Trevor's mom. "Just because it's worth a lot of money?"

"Fifty thousand dollars is more than just a lot of money. Most people don't make that much in a whole year."

"You're stating the obvious," she said. "What do you want to do, sell it?"

"No. It's not ours to sell."

"You're right. It's Trevor's."

"I think he's too young to have something like that in his possession. It's worth too much. It's too much responsibility." Trevor's dad paused. "Maybe we should suggest he give it back to Grandpa," he said softly, trying not to be heard by ears that didn't need to know everything.

"Grandpa wouldn't take it back. He gave it to Trevor for a reason. You know how special Trev is to him."

"I know, but Grandpa didn't know how much it was worth when he gave it to him."

11

"Well he knows now, and he seemed quite pleased about it. Grandpa said, 'Fifty grand for a picture of a man on a piece of paper. The Babe is worth more now than when he played ball.' Then he told Trev to 'take real good care of it.' Right?"

"That's what I'm talking about. I'm not sure Trevor is old enough to take good care of a fifty-thousand-dollar card."

Trevor stood in the hallway, pressed against the wall, listening to his parents' conversation. He couldn't hear every word, but he heard the important ones. He felt a little guilty listening, knowing he shouldn't eavesdrop, but how could he walk away knowing what they were talking about?

Trevor was beginning to understand that this card was more than just a special gift from his great-grandpa. To grown-ups, that card was important because of how much money it was worth—and when money is involved in something, adults start acting funny.

"It *is* a big responsibility," his mother said. "Not many children own something worth that much money. But then again, it is *his* card. We can't take it away from him."

"Then we should suggest that we hold onto it for him. We could put it in a safety deposit box at the bank. Whenever he wants to see it, he's welcome to do so."

"Oh that's convenient," his mother said. "Honey, that just doesn't feel right. The card was a gift to him, so it's his. I say we let *him* take the responsibility for it. If Trevor wants us to put the card in a safety deposit box, then that's what we'll do. We've always taught him to give generously and be responsible with his things, including money. Why should this be any different? I say we explain the value of the card to him, and allow him to make his own decision. It's his to enjoy. Besides, there are only a handful of people who'd actually pay that much for it."

Trevor listened to what his mom and dad each proposed. Trevor knew the card was his, but as he heard his parents' concerns, he really didn't care whether they held it or not. After all, he'd only owned it for one day.

"You're right," his dad said. "It's a big task—but we'll give him ultimate responsibility for it. The bottom line is that we can't take it away from him. We will make one rule though—the card does not leave this house."

Trevor's mom put her arms around her husband and gave him a kiss.

"Good idea. I love when you agree with me," she said. Her eyes locked on his.

"I know you do," he smiled back.

Trevor's mom kissed her husband again.

Oh, man, do they have to do that? he thought as he heard them start to smooch. He retreated to his room, knowing that the card would be his responsibility . . . a *big* responsibility.

He picked up the card from his dresser and looked at 'The Babe.' The photograph showed him in pitching motion. He thought about his great-grandpa standing in the batter's box watching 'The Babe' wind up—and Babe jumping up as his great-grandpa drilled one right between his legs. He couldn't help but laugh out loud.

Then he thought about the card's fifty-thousand-dollar value. *Fifty thousand dollars? That's a lot of money,* he thought.

CHAPTER THREE
The Connection

Mike Tripuka waited for what he felt was an appropriate amount of time to place his call–a polite 24 hours. He'd thought about Trevor and his dad, the card, and their story quite a bit. He couldn't wait to meet a one hundred year-old man who played ball with George Herman, also known as 'Babe' Ruth.

The phone rang. It was Sunday afternoon. Trevor's sister, Kirsten, fielded the call and quickly delivered the phone to her father.

In the back of his mind, Trevor's dad had been hoping this call would not come. He never expected that his grandfather turning one hundred years old two days ago would bring about this kind of attention. He answered the call politely, knowing what Mike wanted. Then he put Mike on hold while he asked his grandfather how he felt about talking to a local reporter about turning one hundred and playing against Babe Ruth many, many years ago.

Trevor's great-grandpa was not the kind of man to turn down a chance to tell his favorite story. Trevor's dad knew this, but he had to ask anyway. Within an hour, Mike Tripuka was sitting on the Mitchell's front porch drinking lemonade and listening to Trevor's great-grandpa tell his amazing story. Trevor and his father sat there, listening too–and they enjoyed every word of it, just as though they were hearing the story for the first time. Stories never seem to get old when they are told with such enthusiasm and passion, two great abilities that Trevor's great-grandfather, Jack Mitchell, possessed.

"The year was 1915," Jack Mitchell began. "It was my rookie year and the first time I ever faced Babe Ruth, who was a rookie the year before. Now, Babe Ruth was a cocky son of a gun. His team, the Red Sox, were good, and he thought that he was the greatest thing to happen to the game since the invention of the baseball, which ended up to be true. Babe *was* great. Everyone knows that. But did you know that there is only one person in the world who ever stole home on him?" Jack Mitchell asked. He loved to set up his story in just the right way.

"It's true," he winked, as Trevor, his father and Mike Tripuka smiled. "And you're looking at him."

At this point, no one who has ever heard the story knows whether to believe him or not. But the fact of the matter is Trevor's great-grandpa never lies. If they kept records back then like they do today, you could look it up.

"You see, although Babe Ruth was a great player, he was also pretty loud and obnoxious," Jack Mitchell said. "I didn't like that about him, and I don't know many folks who did. So I made up my mind that when I heard this guy start to carry on and chatter, I was gonna do something

16

about it. Of course, I didn't know exactly what at the time, but I was determined to do something. This thought occurred to me as I stood in the on-deck circle waiting for my turn at bat.

"Our team was really razzing 'The Babe.' And he had no trouble razzing us back. He used words that made grown men blush. He'd made quite a reputation doing it. When it was my turn at bat, I felt like David against Goliath and I said a little prayer.

"Now, back in those days, I wasn't much of a prayin' man, but I said, 'Lord, this guy is full of pride. Help me put him in his place. If there was ever a time when you felt like answering one of my prayers, I'd be much obliged if you'd do it right now.' " Jack Mitchell paused reflectively. "What happened after that prayer was a series of pretty amazing things. In fact, I'd call it a 'God thing.' "

Mike Tripuka looked at Jack Mitchell with extreme curiosity. He'd never heard anything like this in his life.

" 'The Babe' got two quick strikes on me as I swung and missed two perfectly placed pitches. Then he missed with two balls and the third one almost knocked me right on my derriere.

"With a full count, I prayed again . . . 'Lord, please?'

" 'The Babe' let the ball go, and it came speeding toward me. Then, **BAM!** I hit that sucker up the middle–right between Babe Ruth's legs. He had to do a quick jump in the air so as not to get hit you-know-where. And there I was–standing on first base."

"Nice job!" Mike exclaimed, laughing and smiling from ear to ear.

"But God's blessings didn't end there," Jack Mitchell went on.

"Now, the men in our dugout were really gettin' on Babe's case, which didn't exactly make him happy.

"I took a good lead off first base, and 'The Babe' immediately let me know he was in charge with a quick pick-off move. And he caught me. Silence fell across the stadium. I raced toward second as the first baseman ran me down. He threw the ball to the shortstop waiting at second, and I was caught in a pickle. The shortstop ran at me, and threw the ball back to Babe at first. I took off again toward second, and this time 'The Babe' ran after me.

"With the Good Lord as my witness, what happened next can only be seen as a miracle. I was running so hard and fast that my cap flew off, as caps can do, just moments after 'The Babe' threw the ball to second to get me out. As the ball left Babe's hands heading toward second, it miraculously collided with and landed right in my cap as it flew in the air behind me. And I landed safe and sound at second base."

Mike Tripuka's mouth was wide open. Trevor's father looked at Mike and didn't know what to think. Trevor listened intently; hanging onto his great-grandfather's every word.

"Babe Ruth looked me square in the eye with a look that said, 'You're one lucky duck,' although he probably wouldn't have chosen those exact words.

"Babe proceeded to strike out the next batter with ease. Then, something divine happened once again. As the catcher was throwing the ball back to Babe, I heard a voice. It said one word—softly, but clearly . . . '*Run!*'

"I hesitated for a fraction of a section, then I took off toward third.

"Shocked, the Babe must've seen me out of the corner of his eye, and he threw the ball as fast as he got hold of it over to Mike McNally at third. I slid, and the ump pronounced me 'Safe!'"

At this point, folks who hear this story don't know whether to think Trevor's great-grandpa is just joking around or if he's totally off his rocker. From the expression on Mike's face, he may have been thinking the same thing. Keep in mind, however, that the truth is sometimes stranger than fiction. Trevor's great-grandpa always spoke the truth–and he always gave credit where credit was due. But what will Mike believe?

"It just goes to show there's power in prayer," Mike said, as if reading his mind.

"What happened after that is the reason good ol' Babe Ruth, the Sultan of Swat, the Bambino himself, never forgot my name," he continued with a twinkle in his eye.

"There I was, standing on third. The men on my team were looking at me as if I was someone they'd never seen before. They were all standing up and cheering me on as 'The Babe' got ready to throw his next pitch. I didn't even have time to revel in the moment, because I heard that same voice again: "*Run!*" I didn't know what to think. It was too hard to believe, so I just stood there, dumbfounded, as 'The Babe' threw another strike.

"'Lord, you can't be serious.' I said. He didn't answer, and I didn't hear Him speak again, but a Scripture verse came to my mind. It was something I heard years ago in Sunday school. '*Does God speak and then not act?*' The minute that verse came to me, I knew what I had to do.

"As Babe began his wind-up, I put my trust in the Lord, and I ran! I took off lickety-splicket and ran as fast as I could straight toward home plate.

"There wasn't even time for me to signal the batter, but fortunately he saw me coming and knew not to swing.

"The 90 feet between third base and home plate seemed to take forever. My heart was beating faster east step of the way. Then I fixed my eyes on the goal and began my slide.

"I touched that plate a millisecond before I was tagged by the catcher and the ump yelled 'Saaaaafe!' The crowd went wild, and so did our bench.

"You should've seen the look on Babe Ruth's face. He looked at me as if I'd grown ten legs and three heads! He was definitely humbled. I wish someone had taken a picture of 'The Babe' that I could show you, but I still have it right up here," he said, pointing to his forehead.

"That's the one and only time that anyone ever stole home base off Babe Ruth. I knew that God was me every step of the way on that day, and I know that He's been with me ever since. Of course, He's really been with me since the day I was created, but something clicked that day that really made me believe it. Isn't it wonderful? God is so faithful," he said beaming. "And that's when I discovered that He really does answer prayer."

Trevor's great-grandpa loved to tell that story. Every time he told it, he sounded like a boy again.

Mike paused for a long moment, soaking it all in. "Wow! That is some story," Mike exclaimed, "and you seem to remember everything."

"Like it was yesterday," Trevor's great-grandpa replied.

Mike sipped his lemonade and exchanged a subtle look with Trevor's dad. Mike seemed to be searching for some kind of clue in his eyes–was this for real?

Trevor's dad had a sinking feeling. He never should have let this meeting happen. He only hoped he was right in his initial judgment of the man sipping lemonade before him.

"Wow," Mike said politely. An ever-so-slight tone of disbelief had crept into his voice. "And you held onto the card all these years?"

"Yes. A good friend gave it to me shortly after it happened, and I held onto it."

"And now your great-grandson has it?"

"That's right."

Mike jotted some notes down on his pad, but with a story like this, notes were really not necessary. If ever there was memorable story, this one certainly was.

"Who may I ask is your favorite baseball player?" Mike inquired. He was a sports reporter after all, and sports were his first love.

Jack Mitchell did not hesitate. "Christy Mathewson," he said.

"Now he was a great pitcher," Mike added. "Many people think he's the greatest pitcher of all time. They say he could hit a tin cup from pitching distance. Talk about control."

"Another great thing about Christy Mathewson was that he was a man of strong convictions. Before he entered the big leagues, he promised his mom that he would never pitch a game on Sunday. They called him 'The Christian Gentleman.' Even the reporters loved him. And those reporters could use their pen to make or break you." Trevor's great-grandpa suddenly remembered he was talking to a reporter. "Ah, sorry about that," he chuckled.

"No offense taken," Mike affirmed. "Mr. Mitchell, what do you think is the secret to a long life?"

Jack Mitchell hesitated for a moment and then laughed. "Well, at my age, I've got one foot in the grave and another on a banana peel."

Trevor's dad rolled his eyes. It was a line he's heard his grandpa say at least a thousand times.

"Seriously," Jack went on, "there's no secret to it really. It's a gift. I've done nothing to deserve living this long. With all the things I've done wrong in my life, it's a wonder I'm still here. Every day is a gift, a gift from God . . . whether you're eleven, fifty or one hundred years old."

Mike was writing as fast as he could on his pad, wishing he had tape-recorded the entire conversation. He had prepared a few other questions to ask, but somehow they seemed inappropriate now. He folded his notebook and tucked his pen inside its spiral binding.

"Thank you so much for sharing your story, Mr. Mitchell." Then he looked at Trevor and dad. "Thank you for your time too Mr. Mitchell . . . Trevor. This is an incredible story." He turned his attention to Trevor. "Think you'll ever sell that card, kid?"

"No way," Trevor stated firmly.

"I didn't think so. Thanks again, everyone!" Mike was like a child who just received a new toy and couldn't wait to go home and play with it.

With the interview over, Mike Tripuka was gone.

Trevor's dad still couldn't help but wonder what the future held–and if he did the right thing in welcoming Mike Tripuka into their home.

CHAPTER FOUR

Feeding Frenzy

Mike Tripuka did what every good reporter does when he has a lead on a story–he went home after the interview and continued his research. His first job was to see if there were records of the game that Jack Mitchell talked about. He checked his *Baseball Encyclopedia* and numerous other books of baseball statistics and records. Plenty of records stated Jack Mitchell played in the major leagues, but not one book had anything about the game in question.

He then went on the Internet to see if he could find any information there. Nothing turned up.

His last effort was to call Cooperstown and speak to the librarian at the Baseball Hall of Fame. The story Mike told her sounded familiar, but there were many stories and fables about baseball's golden age–and this was just one of a thousand.

The librarian called Mike back an hour later with news that there were no records about that game in the Hall of Fame Library, "but," she went on to say, "it doesn't mean that the game never happened. There are no records of four games in baseball history from 1911 to 1932. Not even the Hall of Fame has these records. No one knows if these records were stolen, lost or may still be in the basement in some forgotten section of the 'Hall' or in some obscure sports publication."

As a matter of fact, many years earlier, a good friend suggested to Trevor's great-grandfather that maybe "The Babe" himself arranged to have the records of the game "misplaced" so that the game and what happened would be erased from existence, at least on paper anyway.

Mike's piece in the *Suburban Times* was cleverly titled "The Oldest Old-Timer," and appeared in the human-interest section; an area in which Mike Tripuka's writing had never appeared previously. Mike's specialty was sports, but because of the age of the person featured in this story, his editor thought this piece would best serve his publication's audience as a human-interest story.

Trevor's dad wasn't the first person in the family to read the story. That honor went to Trevor's mom who was home when the paper arrived. She immediately called her husband and gave him the news.

Trevor's father rushed home from work. Since he owned and ran the local food market, he had the luxury of leaving if he needed to.

It would be an understatement to say that Trevor's dad was concerned as he read the article, no matter what his wife told him. He wondered what the underlying message of the story would be.

He read the article closely. It was simply the story of a

one hundred-year-old family man who got a hit off and stole home while Babe Ruth was pitching. It went on to tell about the fifty-thousand-dollar card that was a gift to the old-timer's great-grandson. Mike left in the part about the ball colliding with Mr. Mitchell's hat, which gave the piece a comic and magical tone. However, Mike had strategically left out all of the references to Jack Mitchell's prayers, hearing the voice of God and the miraculous events of the day.

The story actually made Jack Mitchell sound like a great baseball player. The fact that the story could not be verified by records was also mentioned toward the end of the article, which could leave the reader with the impression that Trevor's great-grandfather imagined the entire incident. The impact and truth of the story, like many news stories, was determined by the reader's perspective. That aspect of the story did not appeal to Trevor's dad.

Trevor's dad concluded that it could have been much worse. However, a can of worms was already open—and sometimes things have a way of rapidly getting worse before you even realize the worm is out of the can.

Trevor's great-grandfather, on the other hand, was upset that Mike Tripuka didn't include the whole story as he had related it. Since he'd dealt with sports reporters during his entire baseball career, he wasn't too surprised, but he had hoped for more.

The article received great praise from Mike's readers, and numerous letters were written to the paper about the joys of hearing the wit and wisdom that old people have to share. The story was then picked up by the Associated Press and printed in thousands of newspapers around the country. CNN even did a five-minute segment on the story, including an interview with Trevor and his great-grandpa that appeared all over the world. The phone in the Mitchell house rang off the hook for days. Everyone was talking about it, even Trevor's classmates.

Unfortunately, the aftermath of this article would prove to be a time of trial for the entire Mitchell family, especially Trevor.

CHAPTER FIVE

Truth and Consequences

"He's a liar! Your grandpa lies like a rug!" said Frank Carbone, the biggest kid in school. Although he was a bit on the chunky side, Frank was known for being the best player in every sport and an expert when it came to sports statistics and trivia.

"Yeah!" a few other boys agreed.

"He is not, I tell ya! And he's my great-grandfather . . . jerk!" replied Trevor, defending his great-grandpa with every ounce of gusto he could muster. "My great-grandpa would never lie—unlike some people 'round here."

The small crowd watching fell silent as Frank Carbone's eyes grew wider. "Are you calling me a liar?" Frank asked, gritting his teeth and leaning close to Trevor's face.

"Everyone in school knows you lie," Trevor growled. "No one believes what you say. You lied to Mrs. Sikkema last week when she caught you late for class. *You're* the liar." Trevor's passion for his great-grandpa and the truth was clouding his better judgment. His words were provoking the much larger and stronger boy to physical action.

Trevor knew the power of words, too. His father taught him this lesson. He realized he went too far when he saw the fierce anger in Frank's eyes. *Uh oh*, he thought. Trevor's dad always told him that a person's eyes revealed a lot about a person. He was right!

At this point, all eyes on the playground were fixed on Trevor and Frank.

"We're not talking 'bout me, Mitchell. There's no way your great-grandpa stole home off Babe Ruth. There's no record to prove it, even the stupid article said that. He probably never even played against Babe. No records mean there's no proof. I say he's a liar." He leaned in closer. "What are you going to do about it?"

"He's not a liar," Trevor said through his teeth. He was starting to get angry now, too, and he didn't like the feeling.

Everyone waited to see what would happen next. Surely a fight was about to break out. The playground hadn't seen a fight in two weeks, not since Robbie Jones teased Scott Leach about kissing Kim Sanders.

Trevor stood there for a moment contemplating his next move when he remembered something his father had said to him about loving your enemies. He remembered something else too, a story he heard weeks earlier about how we are supposed to turn our cheek when we are struck, and go the extra mile. He didn't really understand the "extra mile" part, but he understood the meaning of the story. Although no one had struck the first blow, he and Frank were certainly hitting one another with words. All of these things swirled through his mind in a flash as his peers gathered around both of them, waiting. Then it occurred to him.

"I'll prove it to you!" Trevor said with authority.

"Yeah, right," Frank fumed.

Trevor bent down and picked up his backpack. He opened the front pocket and slowly pulled out the Babe Ruth card.

"Here. If it never happened, then why would he have this?"

A series of gasps and "Wows" were heard as Trevor held the card for all eyes to see. They heard about its existence, and what it was worth, but they couldn't believe Trevor actually brought the card to school.

There wasn't a boy in the crowd who wouldn't give everything he owned, including his teeth, for *that* card.

At first, Frank Carbone didn't know what to say. Even he was mesmerized by the card's beauty. Then he snapped out of it.

"Old people keep everything. He had it 'cause it was Babe Ruth. What kind of jerk wouldn't keep a Babe Ruth card?"

His reasoning sounded logical to everyone, except Trevor.

"You can think what you like," Trevor said confidently, securing the card in his backpack, "but I'm telling you, my great-grandfather is not a liar. He really did steal home from Babe Ruth. If you want, you can ask him yourself. I'm sure he'd love to tell you *all* about it."

"That's all right. I don't need to hear more lies. I read enough already!" Carbone replied, cocky as ever.

"Good morning, everyone!" It was Mr. Jenkins, the principal.

Trevor was still gritting his teeth after hearing Frank's comment. Then uttered one word, soft enough for just one person to hear it, "Idiot."

Frank Carbone's head whipped around, and he glared

at Trevor. When he saw the principal coming, he casually backed away from Trevor a bit.

"Good morning, everyone!" Mr. Jenkins exclaimed, now in their midst. "Everyone doing all right?"

"Yes, Mr. Jenkins, sir. Everything's . . . great," Frank said confidently.

"The bell should ring any second. Get ready for a great day!"

The small crowd began to disperse. Frank Carbone leaned in toward Trevor. "After school . . . you're dead meat," he said and walked away, followed by four of his pals.

Slowly, the boys began to wander away, returning to their games and conversations.

Great, Trevor thought to himself. *What else could go wrong today?*

Trevor felt a friendly slap on the back. "Cool card, man. Good job." It was Scott Whiteman, but the kids all called him Whitey. Whitey was what Trevor's mom described as a "fair-weather" friend. He only called or hung out with Trevor when there was nothing else to do.

"Thanks," Trevor replied.

"Don't sweat Carbone. He's so dumb that he'd trip over a cordless phone. In fact, I heard that he once tried to put M&M's in alphabetical order," Whitey joked.

His comment caused Trevor to smile for a second. But before Trevor could say another word, Whitey was already running off to catch up with some other friends.

Trevor stood there alone thinking how easy it would have been to insult Frank Carbone more or even to fight with him. Defending his great-grandfather's honor was certainly something worth fighting for, but he knew deep inside that it would have been wrong. This was not the time to fight. His father had been teaching him about honor and loving others. These were more than just words to the members of the Mitchell family. They meant taking action. They were the foundations on which his family lived their lives. His great-grandpa was surely an example of that. As hard as it was to do the right thing, Trevor knew that he was better for it. However, after having resisted the temptation to fight, he was warned and threatened that a fight would occur after school. *I don't want to fight. How did this happen? What am I gonna do?*

The bell rang. Everyone hustled inside.

Trevor adjusted his backpack around his shoulders and walked inside. The thoughts of a dreaded afternoon fight now bombarded him, and even worse, the words Frank Carbone and the others said about his great-grandfather were now planted in his head—and beginning to take root.

The walk home from school that day was excruciatingly long for Trevor. He could have walked with some other boys and girls, but he chose to walk alone. He could even have walked home a different way to avoid the fight, but the fight wasn't the first thing on his mind. His great-grandfather was. He replayed his great-grandpa's story over and over inside his head. It was easy to do since he had heard the story so many times. *It does sound incredible. Maybe they're right. Maybe he did make it up. It is true that there aren't any records to prove it. Not one record . . .*

It was the first time in Trevor's life the thought ever occurred to him. It was the first time he ever doubted his great-grandfather's word, and it left an uneasy feeling in his stomach.

Trevor turned the corner and began to walk down Butternut Avenue. He was two blocks from home now, and

Frank Carbone was nowhere in sight. There were some kids walking about fifty feet behind him and some more on the other side of the street. Trevor could hear them laughing, and he felt as if they were all laughing at him.

He looked to his right and noticed a neighbor, Mrs. Younger, with some groceries. Mrs. Younger was about 65 years old. She had silver hair, and she didn't get around too easily. She had bad arthritis, although she still drove her car. She drove slowly, like many older people, and Trevor heard his dad comment once or twice that it was about time Mrs. Younger gave up her driver's license. She was at her front door, trying to get her key into the lock while holding a bag of groceries. *I wouldn't try that if I were you*, he thought. Then **CRASH!**

Before the key was halfway in the lock, the groceries were on the ground. Mrs. Younger lost her balance trying to catch her groceries and fell on the porch. Instinctively, Trevor dropped his backpack inside her front fence and ran to her aid.

"Are you all right?" Trevor asked, as Mrs. Younger tried to get herself up.

"Yes. I'm fine. I hate all these keys. My fingers aren't as nimble as they used to be. Seems like only yesterday when we didn't need to lock our front doors."

Trevor bent down and helped her pick up her groceries. He picked up a dented can of prune juice, a box of chocolate chip cookies, and a bottle of Gatorade–the orange kind.

"Here," he said, putting the Gatorade into the bag.

The Gatorade was for her 25-year-old son Marshal who recently moved back in with her. Trevor had seen him cutting her lawn a few times.

"Thank you so much," Mrs. Younger said gratefully.

"Hey, I read the article on your grandfather."

"Great-grandfather," Trevor corrected her proudly.

"He's got quite an imagination," she said. "Good story though."

Trevor blinked and stared. He didn't want to get into it with her though.

"Yeah, thanks," he mumbled. "Need anything else?"

"No . . . I'm all right now," she said. "Here, let me give you something for helping me," she added, reaching into her wallet and pulling out a ten-dollar bill.

Trevor saw the ten bucks and was tempted to take it.

"No, you keep it," he said, knowing he shouldn't take money for helping someone. Besides, he knew it was way was too much for what he had done.

"Come on . . . take it," she insisted.

Trevor stuck to his guns and started walking down her front stairs.

"Thanks Mrs. Younger, but you keep it," he yelled.

Trevor looked up at Marshal Younger strolling up the walkway. He was wearing glasses and wore his hair a little past his ear lobes. Marshal handed Trevor his backpack as he passed by.

"Here you go, Sport," he said, as Trevor received the backpack in his chest.

"Thanks," Trevor replied.

"Caught that story on your grandpa . . . that guy is some character," he said, with a tone of voice which told Trevor he didn't believe the story either.

Trevor just smiled and continued on his way. *Doesn't anybody believe Great-grandpa?*

He walked about fifty feet before he spotted Frank Carbone and three of his pals. They were in the distance but on the same side of the street as Trevor. *Oh, no.* Although

Trevor felt a bit afraid, he kept walking. He tried to look around casually behind him. There were still kids walking home from school, but no adults were around. *Lord, help me.*

He decided to just keep walking, calmly, as if this were any other day and he was walking by any other person. He adjusted his backpack and kept a steady pace. He even began to whistle.

Frank Carbone and his friends Jim and Tom saw Trevor coming. They smiled at each other, awaiting their prey. As Trevor got closer and closer, they were stunned to see him looking cool as he started whistling. They looked at one another as if they couldn't believe their eyes. "Doesn't he know why we're here?" Frank asked Jim.

Trevor was right in front of them now. He nodded his head, acknowledged them and walked right on by. He kept on walking and whistling, until . . .

"Hey! Butthead!" That was definitely Frank Carbone's voice.

Do I stop or keep walking?

"Hey, loser with the lying grandfather!"

Trevor stopped. *Great-grandfather. Can't anyone get that right?* Then he slowly turned around.

"What?" Trevor asked, matter-of-factly.

"What do you mean 'what'? You heard me this morning. I said you were gonna be dead meat, and I meant it."

Trevor had to think fast, again. "Why?"

"Huh?" Frank said, caught off guard.

"Why do you want to fight?" Trevor added.

"Mitchell. Are you forgetting something? You called me an idiot, remember? I don't let anyone call me an idiot. Got it?" He was walking closer to Trevor.

"Listen, Frank, you can hit me if you want, but you know what I'm gonna do?"

"Cry, probably," he laughed. The other boys were laughing, too.

A small crowd of kids who were walking home stopped and began to gather around, one of which was Trevor's friend Ginger.

"Why don't you leave him alone, Frank?" Ginger said. "You're such a bully. You think you're just so cool."

"You gonna fight his battles?" Frank giggled, turning to his pals. "He needs a girl to fight his battles!" With those words, Frank charged and pushed Trevor hard. Trevor stumbled backwards. His backpack fell off his shoulder and slid down his arm into his hand. "You want her to fight for ya . . . baby?" Frank said provokingly. He moved forward and pushed Trevor again. This time Trevor fell down, causing him to release the backpack. It landed near Jim and Tom.

"Leave him alone, Frank!" Ginger yelled. "Don't you think you're a little bigger than he is? It's not a fair fight. Or is that too much for your little brain to understand?"

"Hey!" Trevor shouted. He was standing up now, dusting his pants off. "Don't you wanna know what I'm gonna do if you hit me?"

Everyone was a little stunned, especially Frank and his friends.

"Yeah . . . what?" Carbone asked in his toughest voice.

Trevor waited a moment. Everyone stared at him.

"Nothing," he said. "I'm not going to do a single thing. You can hit me and hit me again, and you know what? I'm still not gonna do anything. Not because I'm afraid, but because I don't wanna fight."

Frank looked at him strangely. He never heard anything like this before, neither had anyone else. Trevor had no idea where he was mustering up the courage to say the words that came out of his mouth.

"If my calling you an idiot made you so mad, then I'm sorry. So go ahead . . . beat me up. Come on . . . get it over with. We all have things to do."

Frank froze. He wasn't sure quite what to do. All eyes were on him awaiting his next move. He moved closer toward Trevor. "All right, Mitchell. I'll teach you to call me an idiot." He clenched his fist, pulled back his hand and threw a punch at Trevor. Just before his fist connected with Trevor's face, he stopped. Frank laughed as Trevor flinched.

"Hah!" Frank yelled. "What a loser! I still say your grandfather's a liar. I have two words for you, loser: *no records.*" He laughed again, causing his friends to laugh, too. "You're both whackos!" He turned to his friends. "Come on. Let this baby go home to his mommy and grandpa!"

Jim was now holding Trevor's backpack. He passed it to Tom who shoved it into Trevor's chest. "Here. Have a nice day, Mitchell," Tom said.

Then the boys left, and everyone else went on their way back home, too–except Ginger.

"What a jerk," Ginger muttered. "I can't believe that guy." Ginger's eyes searched Trevor's face. "Are you all right?"

"Yeah," Trevor said, tucking his shirt in and adjusting his backpack firmly onto his shoulders. "I'm all right." He smiled. "Thanks for sticking up for me. But you do realize you almost made things worse, don't you?"

"I would've kicked his butt," Ginger said jokingly and held her hand up for a high five.

Trevor laughed and hit her hand high. "He's a big enough target," he joked. Ginger laughed.

CHAPTER SIX
Double-Minded

No records. What if the game never really happened? What if Great-grandpa did make it all up? The words swirled around and around in his head. Now that his troubles with Frank Carbone were behind him, Trevor couldn't get his mind off all the words that everyone said. He became so dazed and locked in thought that he didn't even see or hear the neighbor's dog barking at him as he walked slowly to his house.

Trevor came through his front door, took off his backpack and put it in its usual spot on the stairs.

He walked inside quietly. He didn't want to talk to his great-grandpa right now. He had too many questions. *Please, let him be taking a nap,* he thought.

He saw his great-grandpa sitting in his chair. His eyes were closed. *Yes! He's asleep.* Trevor looked again carefully to make sure that he was breathing. This had become a habit for Trevor. Sometimes when he entered a room where his great-grandpa was napping, he would start to stare at his chest to make sure air was coming in and going out.

Trevor watched him for a moment, waiting for his chest to fill in and out with air. *Good, still breathing.* Trevor was relieved.

Then he looked at his great-grandpa differently. *Why would you make that story up? You wouldn't lie to me, would you? To everyone? Why would you do that?*

He studied his great-grandpa more closely, looking at his thick snow-white hair, not realizing that a full head of hair is rare at age one hundred. He noticed the large brown spots on his great-grandpa's hands. Trevor's great-grandpa was in unbelievably good shape for a man who just turned one hundred. There are men twenty-five-years-old who don't have his great-grandpa's love for life. There are also men in their seventies who don't have his great-grandpa's physical and mental strengths. Except for eyeglasses and an undetectable hearing aid, his great-grandpa was a man blessed with long life and good health.

On his lap sat his Bible. Great-grandpa's Bible was practically falling apart, not because it was old, which it was. There are plenty of old Bibles that still look brand new. His great-grandpa's Bible looked old because it was well used. "You can always tell if a man has his act together by whether or not his Bible is falling apart," is what Trevor's great-grandpa always said.

Trevor hated how he was feeling inside. He always believed anything and everything his great-grandpa told him. *Could my Great-grandpa be a liar? I need to talk to someone. But, who?*

His friends at school all believed Frank Carbone. Trevor's sister, Kirsten, was older and too wrapped up in her own life to really care how he felt. His best friend in the neighborhood was Ginger, but she hated sports, especially baseball. She didn't even have any grandparents that were still living. *She'd never understand.* His father was at work. *I don't want him to know I'm even thinking this way.*

That left one person in Trevor's world to talk to–Mom.

"The kids at school are calling Great-grandpa a liar. No one believes it's true. No one believed it happened," Trevor said.

"Kids your age love to pick on each other; we've talked about that, honey. Don't let it bother you. That's exactly what they want. The more they see that their teasing upsets you, the more they're gonna do it." She stroked Trevor's hair. "That's one thing your father and I never wanted you or your sister to do is tease another child. As far as we know, you've both been pretty good about resisting that temptation, right?"

"I have, Mom," Trevor assured her. "But . . . "

"But what?" she asked with a warm smile.

"But what if they're right? What if Great-grandpa did make it all up?"

Trevor's question was sincere; he needed to ask it. He needed to know from someone older–someone with more wisdom about it.

"I mean, there aren't any records to prove it," Trevor professed. "Even the article said that. So maybe he did. Maybe Great-grandpa made it all up."

Trevor noticed his mom look over his shoulder. He turned his head and looked into the eyes of his great-grandpa. What he saw is something he'd never forget. Great-grandpa's eyes looked sad and his mouth was turned down.

"I was just wondering where you put my glasses?" Jack Mitchell asked.

"They're on the table next to your chair," Trevor's mom answered.

Great-grandpa slowly looked down and shook his head. He didn't say another word. Then he looked back up at Trevor before he walked away.

Trevor quickly looked back at his mom. She took a deep breath, not knowing exactly what to say.

Tears filled his eyes as he looked back at her. *I'm sorry. What do I do?* his eyes pleaded.

She sighed, not having an immediate answer. She knew Jack Mitchell well–well enough to know that he was very hurt.

"This has to be the worst day of my life," Trevor said.

"Things are not always easy, are they?" his Mom said, not knowing the half of it.

"Tell me about it," Trevor replied. He got up off her bed and walked out of the room.

There was only one thing on Trevor's mind now–the card. He wanted to see it again. He desperately wanted to believe. He headed for the stairs and picked up his backpack. As he did, Trevor looked outside and noticed his great-grandfather sitting on the stoop. His head was down and his eyes watery. But Trevor didn't know what to say or do, so he quietly made his way up the stairs toward his room.

Trevor sat down on his bed, quickly unzipped the front pocket of his backpack and reached inside. The card was gone!

CHAPTER SEVEN
Rewind

Panic! *Where is it? I don't believe this!* Trevor turned the pack upside down and dumped its contents onto the bed. He shook the pack violently, making sure nothing could stay inside.

He couldn't scream or yell, although he wanted to. Nobody could know what happened. *Where is it? Think! Think! When was the last time I had it? School. I should have never brought it to school. I should have just . . . I had it last at the end of school. I was at my desk putting my books in . . . and it was still there. Then it should be here!*

He rifled through the bag's contents on his bed. He opened every book, moved every item. All he saw were three spiral notebooks, a math book, pens, pencils, erasers, a pack of Big League Chew®, some empty Zip-Lock bags and a Granola bar left over from lunch.

Maybe it fell out? He wanted to scream. He checked the zipper on his backpack to see if it was broken. It worked fine.

I should have never taken it out of the house! I lost my great-grandpa's Babe Ruth card!

He knew his parents were forgiving people. Then he remembered how much his dad didn't want him to have the card in the first place. It was worth a ton of money, and they trusted him with the card. *Great-grandpa had it for practically eighty years, and I lost it in a week.* He didn't even want to think how his great-grandpa would feel–as if he didn't already feel bad enough. The card was a family heirloom and he had entrusted it to him.

I'm in the biggest trouble I've ever gotten myself into. I've gotta find it!

Then he remembered that three other people had their hands on his backpack. *Maybe it was stolen. Marshal had it. So did Jim Evans and Tom Murphy. Did one of them take it? But why? They wouldn't . . . they couldn't. Who could possibly be that mean! Then again, maybe it just fell out. I should look before I accuse anyone. Besides, they just couldn't have taken it. Oh, man!*

Trevor put on his baseball cap, looked down at the floor and backtracked his every step–every place that he and that backpack had been.

He checked the hallway and the stairway. Nothing.

"Bye, mom! I'm going out!" he yelled, his voice cracking. He was out the door in a flash.

He looked everywhere. His yard, the sidewalk–all along his route home from school and its surrounding areas. Anywhere and everywhere the card could have fallen, he looked.

He was thankful he didn't have to worry about the card blowing away. Its heavy plastic protective case would ensure that it stayed wherever it landed. *If it landed,* he thought.

He walked down the block and stopped at Mrs. Younger's house. *This is the only place I stopped, the only place I put the bag down.* He looked under the bushes inside Mrs. Younger's fence. It wasn't there.

He looked along her walkway just as Mrs. Younger opened her front door.

"Everything all right, Trevor?" she yelled.

Do I tell her what I'm looking for? He paused. *No, I can't.* "Yeah," he yelled. "Just looking for something!"

"What are you looking for?" she yelled back.

"Umm . . . nothing special . . . don't worry about it."

"All right. Whatever it is, I hope you find it." Then she closed the door.

Marshal came home as I was leaving. He handed me my backpack. He had a chance to take it. Trevor immediately looked in the driveway for Marshal's car. It was gone.

All right. Calm down. I have a suspect. I have three. First, I have to finish backtracking my steps before I jump to conclusions.

So, that's what Trevor did. He turned the corner and traced every step of the way back to school, looking everywhere on the ground for the card. He even got the janitor to let him back into the building so he could check his path back to his desk. The card was nowhere to be found.

A lump formed in Trevor's throat, and he felt like he was going to cry. He started to, but stopped himself.

He was mad . . . at himself, for taking the card to school. *I had to, though. It was so cool, and everyone wanted to see it.* Then he got scared, scared of what might happen to him.

As soon as he got out of the school building, he ran home, desperately trying to hold back his tears.

CHAPTER EIGHT
The Pickle

Trevor dreaded going inside his house. He knew his sister, Kirsten, would be home from school by now. She got home later than usual because of cheerleading practice. He had to act calm, as if everything were normal.

Act normal, he told himself over and over. It was a lot easier said than done. He was still holding back his tears as he went inside.

Great-grandpa, Kirsten, and his mom were sitting together in the living room talking. He walked through the door and immediately had six eyes staring at him. He was a little out of breath from running, and his eyes were red. He didn't know what to say.

"Hi, honey," said his mom. "Where'd you go in such a hurry?"

"Umm. School. I forgot something I needed for class tomorrow." He lied. *I can't believe I just did that.* Now he was as bad as Frank Carbone was. He hated lying to his mother–to anyone. The first time he lied to his mother he was eight and came home with green paint stains on his pants. His mother asked him what had caused the stains.

He said he was playing baseball, and it was a new kind of green dirt. The truth was that some older boys had talked him and his friend, Scott, into playing near a water tower where he wasn't allowed to play. The paint was from a fence he climbed to get there. *I lied then to stay out of trouble, too*, he thought.

His lie was more believable now than then. After all, who ever heard of green baseball dirt? Now his lies were getting better, and he didn't like the fact that he sounded so believable.

His mother looked at him strangely, because he didn't have a book or anything in his hand. Maybe he wasn't such a good liar after all.

"Uhhh . . . I'm gonna go up to my room for a while," Trevor said waving to Kirsten, his mom and great-grandpa. On his way up the stairs, he casually looked again at his great-grandpa who would not make eye contact with him. But right now, that was the least of his problems.

"He's so weird," Kirsten commented. "Are you sure he's related to me?" she said with a typical teenage attitude.

Trevor's mom didn't question her son's statement, though her motherly instinct told her something was up.

Trevor sat on his bed with his head between his knees. He had no clue where the card could be. *Was it stolen? What if it wasn't stolen? What if I really lost it?* Trevor couldn't take it. He was scared and started to cry.

He tried hard to hold back the tears, but they welled up inside him until they just burst out and overflowed. He tried to cry quietly. *Dad will be home soon.* The thought of that did not make Trevor feel any better.

Trevor dried his tears with his shirtsleeve and blew his nose. He hit his pillow as hard as he could, and then sat on his bed with his head down and his hands over his eyes.

What do I do? His brain felt like it would explode. He didn't have many options. He quickly got up and paced around his room.

I could call the cops. Or maybe I should put "Lost" signs all around the neighborhood. Then everyone would know, including Mom, Dad and Great-grandpa–not to mention the kids at school. This is one huge mess. Kirsten's teasing him for being such a lame brain was nothing compared with the problems he had now.

He looked again at the backpack. *It couldn't have fallen out.* This led him back to Marshal Younger, Jim Evans and Tom Murphy. *It could have been stolen. They were the only other people to touch my bag. Should I ask them if they took it? What if they didn't? How would I feel being accused of something like that? And what if they did do it? Did I really think they would just admit it? Maybe I should tell Mom and Dad.* Trevor thought long and hard. *No. I have to solve this myself.*

That left him with one option–investigate. *I'll start with the first person who had my bag–Marshal Younger.*

Trevor slipped back out of his house undetected. He stood outside the Younger house, replaying the day's events in his mind. He looked on the ground again to make doubly sure the card wasn't there. Then he looked in the driveway–Marshal's car was back. *What do I say?* This was serious. The only person he'd ever accused of anything before was his sister.

He wished he wasn't alone, but this was something he had to do by himself. In any other circumstance, if something this important had been taken from him, he'd have his mom or dad with him for support. He brought his mom with him five years earlier to his friend Ginger's house when she had broken his pinwheel and wouldn't give it back. *I knew Ginger had my pinwheel,* he thought. *But I don't know if Marshal has the card. Yet I have to find out ... and soon!*

How do I do this? Trevor's finger slowly moved to ring the doorbell. It rang. *No turning back now.* Seconds later the door opened, revealing Marshal himself.

"Hey, Sport," Marshal said in a friendly, innocent and welcoming manner. "What can I do for ya? You want my mom?"

"No. I, uhhh, want to talk to you." Trevor looked away, then back at Marshal. "I was wondering . . . I lost something earlier today and ... umm . . . I thought you might have found it. I lost it back there." He pointed to where his backpack had been.

"Sorry, little guy. I didn't find anything. What was it? If I find it, I'll let you know."

"Oh nothing . . . don't worry about it. I . . . I gotta go." Trevor turned and quickly walked away.

He sounded like he was telling the truth. But most liars are good at that. If he stole it, why would he give it back anyway? Trevor groaned. *I should have just asked him if he took the card while I had the chance.* Trevor knew deep inside that he just couldn't do that. A tear welled up in his eye again, and he quickly swiped it away as it rolled down his cheek.

Trevor ran back to his room. He successfully avoided all conversation on his way into the house. His dad would be home soon. He tried to take matters into his own hands with no success, but there were still two more suspects. Yet he knew he couldn't accuse them. He just couldn't go after them now. He was scared and he needed help, but who on earth could help him? The only answer was to tell his parents. He was caught in a one big pickle.

Oh, no.

CHAPTER NINE
First Things Last

"You lost it?" his father barked. He was not happy.

"Dad . . . shhhhh . . . I don't want Great-grandpa to know."

"Honey," Trevor's mom said, trying to calm her husband.

"He's gonna have to know," said Mr. Mitchell as his hands flew up in the air in frustration. He was trying hard to control his anger.

Trevor's eyes widened with fear. *Please don't tell Great-grandpa!*

"Yes, but he doesn't have to know this minute." Trevor's father took a deep breath and tried to calm down. "Now tell us everything again, slowly. What happened?"

Trevor told them the whole story again—about bringing the card to school, his great-grandpa being called a liar, and showing all the kids the card. He admitted what happened on the way home, as he helped Mrs. Younger and Marshal handed him his backpack. Then he told his parents about the near fight with Frank Carbone, and how Jim and Tom handed him his pack and he discovered that the card was gone. He described his attempts to backtrack every move he'd made. Then he told his parents about going back to see Marshal.

"You didn't accuse him, did you, honey?" his mom asked, looking concerned.

"No. I just asked him if he found anything."

"How'd he react?" Trevor's father inquired.

"He acted like he didn't know what I was talking about. He said if he found something, he'd let me know."

They were all sitting on the bed in his parent's bedroom; it was tense and quiet. No one really knew what to say or what to do.

"Trev, what do you want me to do? I can't go to the Younger's or Jim and Tom's parents and accuse them of stealing the card. I can't call the police and ask them to do it either because there is no evidence. You didn't see any of them take the card, right?"

"No."

"Then I can't accuse them. Are you sure you didn't lose it?"

A tear ran down Trevor's face. "I don't know. I went back. I traced my steps. I couldn't find it. I'm sorry. I'm so sorry." Trevor's crying turned into sobs. His mom embraced him in her arms. She gently and lovingly stroked his hair as she looked at her husband. Neither parent was sure exactly what to do.

"Tell you what . . . your father and I will walk back with you," his mother said. "We'll look, too. Three pairs of eyes should be able to find it if it's still out there. Okay?"

Trevor was sniffling now. He had his tears back under control.

"All right," he said, still choked up.

"Hey . . . what's all the hubbub about in here?" It was his great-grandpa.

Trevor looked at his father.

"Nothing to worry about Grandpa. Everything's all right," Trevor's dad said.

Great-grandpa looked at Trevor. Even though he was still hurt, he didn't like seeing his great-grandson upset. "Anything I can do to help?"

"No. We have it covered for now. Thanks though, Grandpa," Trevor's father said.

Great-grandpa didn't push the matter any further. He knew when to stay out of parenting business. "All right," he said. "If you need me, you know where to find me." Then he walked away.

"Thank you," Trevor said, taking a deep breath. He felt a little better, with a lot of emphasis on the word *little*.

"Okay, let's get going. We need a chance to find the card and think some more before we worry Grandpa," Mr. Mitchell said. "So . . . are you ready? Shall we start the hunt?"

"This is important. I think we could use one more set of eyes for this," said Trevor's mom. Trevor looked at her curiously. "I really think we should take Kirsten along."

"Oh, mom," Trevor whined. "No. No way. I don't want her to know. She'll never let me live it down."

"Trev. You know how good she is at finding things."

"Yeah, but . . ."

"Your mother's right," Trevor's dad added. "I'll make sure she doesn't tease you. She's old enough to understand how important this is. I agree with your mother." He started to chuckle. "That kid can find anything."

"But Dad . . . I don't want the kids at school to find out. If she knows the whole school will be talking about it."

"I'll make her promise not to tell anyone," his father assured him. "She'll keep her word. You can trust her, Trev."

Trevor thought hard for a second. *I can't believe I'm saying this.* "All right. But she better not say anything . . . to anyone."

They all walked together–Trevor, his mom, his dad and Kirsten–backtracking Trevor's steps home from school and looking at the ground as they walked.

Great-grandpa stayed at home. He felt a little left out when they didn't ask him to come for their "walk," but their mission couldn't include him right now.

The Mitchells searched every square inch along the sidewalk. They moved branches, looked behind fire hydrants, inspected flower beds, searching anywhere and everywhere the card might have fallen.

"I bet we look pretty silly to the neighbors," Kirsten joked.

Her comment caused everyone to laugh, even Trevor.

They continued looking, following Trevor's path home.

"Trev," his father asked. "How come you did this by yourself before coming to us?"

"I wanted to make sure it was lost."

"And . . ." his father added.

"And I was scared. I didn't want to get in trouble."

"You even went and talked to Marshal Younger without your mom and me."

"I know. I'm sorry."

"I'm glad you're sorry, but more importantly, I want you to know you can always come to us when you have a problem. Okay? Don't be afraid." Trevor's dad locked eyes with his son. "I owe you an apology, too. I was only thinking about the dollar value of the card when I got angry. I didn't think about how you were feeling. I'm sorry too."

"That's okay, Dad. I know this is all my fault. I never should have taken the card out of the house in the first place. *I'm really* sorry."

"Well, you're right about that. You did break a rule, and we'll talk about that later. For now, the fact that the card is gone is punishment enough . . . for all of us. I just want you to come to us first next time. All right?"

"You, too, Kirsten," Trevor's mom said.

"Oh I will!" she affirmed.

"You know, kids, adults do the same thing sometimes. When we have a problem, we try to do everything ourselves to solve the problem before we bring it to the Lord. We all need to remember to go to God for help *first.*"

"Believe me, Dad, I've been praying big time," Trevor exclaimed.

The Mitchell family went to school and back, searching every inch of the way. Unfortunately, when they returned to their front walkway, they were still empty-handed.

Trevor wanted to cry again, but his mom, dad and Kirsten reassured him everything would be all right. They all prayed together that the Lord would somehow help bring the card back to them.

That night, it rained hard outside. Under normal circumstances, Trevor would have been watching the baseball game on television with his great-grandpa, but Trevor didn't want to be near him now. He couldn't face him, not with everything that had happened in the past eight hours. Instead, Trevor sat by his bedroom window and watched the thunderstorm, thinking that if the card was out there; it would surely ruined by now. *Not even the plastic case would protect it from rain like this.*

CHAPTER TEN

Hardball

The bell rang indicating the start of recess, and all the sixth-graders at Calvin Coolidge Elementary School took over the playground. Trevor exited the school alone. He only had one thing on his mind now–the investigation. He still had two more suspects he wanted to question.

He had watched enough detective shows on television to know that finding out the right answers also meant asking the right questions–and talking to the right people. He had his suspects–Jim Evans and Tom Murphy. He had a motive. Now, he just needed to find out if his hunches were right.

Where do I start? I can't just come out and ask them. I have to be sneaky. I also stink at being sneaky. I should have paid more attention to all those detective shows.

Trevor looked around the playground and spotted Jim Evans. *Good. He's alone. Where's Frank?* Trevor perused the kickball game and the basketball court. *There he is, playing basketball. Oh, no. Tom is with him. I'll deal with him later.* Frank scored a basket and started dancing around, rubbing his skill into the other kids' faces. Frank was cocky all right. *Lord, please help me find this card,* Trevor thought to himself. He quickly looked around for Jim again. He was still alone, but heading for the field. *This may be my only chance.*

"Hey, Jim!" Trevor shouted, running up to him.

Jim turned around and looked at Trevor with an expression that seemed to say, *why are you calling me?*

"Hey, how's it going?" asked Trevor, trying to act non-chalant.

"Good," Jim said, looking as if he'd been asked a nuclear physics question. "What do you want?"

"Me? Oh, nothing really . . . I was just wondering . . . umm . . . do you collect baseball cards?" Trevor winced, but looked intensely at Jim's face for a reaction. *Uh oh! He was too obvious. How stupid. Think Trevor, think!*

"Yeah, of course I do. Who doesn't?" Jim replied. "Why do you wanna know, Mitchell?"

"No reason. It's just that I started collecting cards a while back. I thought that maybe you and I could trade cards sometime. You know, maybe you can show me your collection sometime." Trevor looked closely at Jim's face to see if he showed any sign of guilt or suspicion.

"I don't think so. Your collection's definitely better than mine," he said, referring to the Babe Ruth card. "I only have new stuff." Jim paused a moment, then the business-man inside of him came out. "But . . . I'm always willing to trade some doubles. Do you have any Yankees?"

Trevor was still looking into Jim's eyes for a sign, any sign, that Jim was the one who had his precious card.

"Hello . . . are you listening, Mitchell?" Jim said, shaking his head.

"Umm. Yeah. Yeah. I've got some Yankees. I even have doubles."

56

"Cool. Then maybe we can do a trade sometime."

"Hey! Can we get a little help here?" It was one of the kids from the kickball game. The ball had shot over to where Jim and Trevor were standing.

"Come on, Jim! Get in the game!" one of the boys yelled. Jim picked up the red playground ball and threw it back to the other kids.

"Gotta go, Mitchell! Hey, when we trade, can you bring that Babe Ruth card? I'd sure like to see it again!" he shouted running onto the field.

"Uh . . . sure!" Trevor answered, knowing that if the card ever were returned to him, he'd never ever take it out of his house again.

Man, this is hard. It's a lot harder than it looks on TV. Jim looked sincere though. He didn't flinch one bit when I asked to see his collection. What if he was onto me? Maybe he asked to see the card to try to throw me off? What do I do now?

Trevor turned around just in time to see Ginger.

"Hey, Ginger!" he called. *Private Eye Rule Number 101 ...always look for witnesses.*

"No, I didn't see anything," Ginger answered. "Why?"

"No reason. I just thought that maybe you might have seen something 'illegal' happen during the fight," Trevor told her. "You didn't see anyone take anything . . . from anyone . . . did you?"

"No. Why do you ask? And why are you being so weird about it? This is me, remember? What's up?"

"Nothing. Nothing's up," Trevor said half-convincingly.

"I know you, Trevor Mitchell. I can tell when something's wrong. What is it? Maybe I can help."

"Seriously, nothing's wrong. I'm... I'm all right," Trevor stuttered. "Maybe I can tell you later."

"Fine, be that way," Ginger said. Trevor could tell that her feelings were a little bent out of shape. "I just thought we were friends."

"We are."

"But yet you're keeping secrets from me. Fine, see if I care," she said walking away.

"Ginger! Come on!" Trevor yelled, but she didn't turn back. Trevor shook his head and looked down at the ground. *I'm not doing very well. I sure could use some help. I'm gonna bust if I don't tell someone soon. So why didn't I just tell her then? Probably because she can't keep a secret.*

Trevor looked up and noticed his friend Whitey playing stickball with a couple guys. On any normal day, Trevor would be playing, too. Stickball was a great way to practice your swing for baseball. Trevor watched enviously for a moment, longing to play, but he didn't have time to do that right now. *I really do need some help. But who can I trust?* He looked over at Whitey. *Whitey can keep a secret. He never told anyone I kissed Jennifer Abbott last semester. And he knows everybody.*

Trevor walked over to where the boys were playing stickball, called time out, took Whitey aside and told him everything. Whitey's job was to be Trevor's eyes and ears. Whitey would be "the informer" if he heard anything suspicious.

Whitey wasn't really interested in helping Trevor, which was pretty typical for Whitey. He didn't like to go out of his way for anyone. He was friends with lots of kids because he was like a chameleon, changing his personality according to the crowd he was hanging around. *At least my secret is safe with him,* Trevor thought. Plus, Trevor was running out of options. He had to find that card!

The stickball game resumed–still without Trevor.

Instead, he turned his attention to the basketball court where Tom Murphy was shooting hoops.

"Excuse me! Trevor! Trevor Mitchell!"

Oh no. It was Mr. Jenkins, the principal. *What does he want? Doesn't this guy ever work?* "Uh, yes, sir?" Trevor answered.

"I've been looking for you. I have a great idea that I'm sure you're gonna love."

Trevor looked at him curiously.

"Our guest speaker for Friday's assembly canceled on me this morning. At first, I was very upset. Then I remembered you."

"Me?"

"Yes. I remembered you and your grandfather . . ."

"Great-grandfather," Trevor interjected, somewhat annoyed.

"Oh yes, your *great*-grandfather. I think it would be wonderful if he would come to the assembly Friday and talk to everyone about playing in the major leagues and of course about playing with Babe Ruth. I just love that story. He was great on CNN, so were you!"

"Thanks," Trevor said with very little enthusiasm.

"I'm sure everyone would just love it—and it would sure help me out, if you know what I mean?" he said softly.

Trevor stood there frozen. *I think that's the worst idea I ever heard in my life.*

"Umm. I don't know. He's pretty busy," Trevor answered awkwardly.

"Can you ask him?" Mr. Jenkins said, noticing the look of uneasiness on Trevor's face. "Or perhaps I should call your parents and ask them myself. That would probably be best now, wouldn't it?"

"I . . . I'm not sure . . ." Trevor stammered. "I . . ."

"Oh! And of course, we'd love for you to bring the card. That would be so awesome," he said, trying to be cool. "Wouldn't it? I heard you had it here yesterday. I'd really like to see it. Do you happen to have it with you now?"

"Uh, no. No, I don't."

"That's all right. Thanks, Trevor. This is just great. I'll call your house tonight. This will be a very memorable assembly. Well, the bell should be ringing soon. Study hard. Study, study, study, that's what I always say. See you later."

"Yeah, sure . . . bye," Trevor said softly as Mr. Jenkins walked away.

Memorable? You're not kidding. What a week! No one believes Great-grandpa. They'll all laugh at him. I can't let that happen. All this because of that stupid card.

CHAPTER ELEVEN
Cut-off Play

Trevor stood in his kitchen and told his mom about the principal's request, then blurted out, "Mom, you can't let him speak to the class. They'll laugh at him! *Please*, when Mr. Jenkins calls you, don't answer, or say he's not here. Say he went on a trip or something. Say anything, just don't let Great-grandpa speak at that assembly," Trevor pleaded.

"Honey, I can't lie to Mr. Jenkins. Grandpa didn't go away. He's right here," his mother gently said.

"Then just don't give Great-grandpa the call. He'll say yes. He doesn't know about the card. He . . ."

"He's still pretty hurt, Trev. He may not even want to do it, even if they do ask him."

There was a long pause. Trevor looked down at the floor. He didn't know what to do or say anymore.

"You two still haven't made up. You've never gone this long not talking to him. You can't avoid him forever, you know."

"But Mom . . . I just don't know what to do . . . what to think."

"What *do* you think?" his mother asked.

"I just told you. I don't know." Trevor took a deep breath. He sat down, put his elbows on the kitchen table and cupped his chin in his hands.

"Life is never simple, is it Trev?"

"Tell me about it," Trevor replied.

"Trev let me tell you something about people . . . and life, for that matter. People are sometimes the hardest things to understand. I'll admit that when I first heard your great-grandpa's story, I thought that maybe he had an overactive imagination. Especially when he got to the part about hearing God say, 'Run.' For a while, I wondered if maybe he felt guilty for humbling Babe Ruth that day, so he needed to shift credit to a higher power. Then, as I got to know him better, I knew that he was a man of his word who had no reason to lie. Most men would brag about it and say it was all their own doing and how great they were. Your great-grandpa always says that what happened was by the grace of God. Sometimes with people, and with life, we just have to take things on faith. I believe Grandpa's story."

"You do?"

"Very much. It's all right to question things; that's how we learn and grow. That's how we discover truth. Just don't let your mind or heart be ruled by doubt. You have to choose what you are going to believe and what you're not. Then there are some things that you just have to take on faith. Do you understand?"

Trevor didn't answer right away. He was still process-ing his mother's words. Then he smiled. "Yeah," he said feeling better. "I do."

"Blessed are those who have not seen and yet have believed, right?"

"That's right," he said, grasping the connection. "But what about Great-grandpa? I hurt his feelings . . . and Principal Jenkins is gonna call about the assembly. And the card is gone. This is a mess."

"What do you think you should do?" she asked.

Trevor approached his great-grandfather timidly. He hated the way he was feeling. His stomach was in knots.

Great-grandpa was sitting in his chair doing a little channel surfing. He saw Trevor out of the corner of his eye but didn't acknowledge him. As old and wise as he was, he was still human and a bit stubborn. His word had been questioned by one of his favorite people. In a way, Trevor had called him a liar, and being called a liar at any age is never a good thing.

"Great-grandpa?" Trevor said. *He must hate me*, Trevor thought. "Great-grandpa?"

Jack Mitchell turned and acknowledged Trevor's presence.

"Hello, Trevor," he said. There was no usual smile or hug.

"Great-grandpa . . . I want you to know . . . that I'm... I'm sorry for what I said the other day."

"You're sorry I heard you," he said back honestly.

Trevor paused. "No," Trevor answered. "I'm really sorry for what I said . . . and for what I was thinking. I didn't mean to doubt you. I just did. I don't know what came over me. I'm really, super sorry. I didn't want to hurt your feelings." Trevor didn't know what else to say.

His great-grandfather turned the TV off and looked at Trevor. He could tell the little boy standing before him was sincere in his apology. He also understood how some people might think his story was a little "out there." Jack Mitchell also knew that when someone sincerely says, "I'm sorry," the next step must be forgiveness.

"Come here, Trev . . . your apology is accepted." He opened his arms and slowly embraced his great-grandson. His arms were shaking a bit, and it took a second for him to pull Trevor in close.

"I love you, Great-grandpa,"

"I love you, too, Trev. You're the apple of my eye, you know that?"

Trevor smiled looking into his great-grandpa's eyes. He looked relieved.

His mother watched the whole thing through the living room door. She smiled, clasping her hands and winking at her son. There is something special about hearts and lives being reconciled. It's the kind of thing that causes angels to rejoice in heaven.

Trevor removed himself from the embrace.

"There's something else I want you to know, okay? I *do* believe you, Great-grandpa. I really do."

"That's okay, Trev. I imagine Daniel's great-grandson had a hard time believing his great-grandpa survived the den of lions. I understand."

Trevor's great-grandfather held up his hand for a high five, and Trevor hit it. "Do you want to watch the ball game with me tonight?" he asked. "Hasn't been the same without you."

"Yeah, definitely!" Trevor replied, pleased to be on good terms with his great-grandpa again.

"Maybe we can even play a little catch later?" Great-grandpa smiled. "We can work on that fielding of yours. You're good, but if you wanna make it to the big leagues, you gotta practice. Yeah . . . I think a catch is just what we need. I've missed that, too."

"Great-grandpa . . ." Trevor said with a huge smile. "I hope I can do everything you can do when I'm your age."

"You're already halfway there, Sport," Jack Mitchell replied with a wink and a chuckle.

Trevor glanced through the door at his mom who was smiling at him. He smiled back. But there was still more that Trevor had on his mind.

"Umm, Great-grandpa?" Trevor said timidly.

"Yes?"

"There's something else I need to tell you . . ." Trevor looked again at his mom whose eyes told him to go ahead. "Uh . . . it's about the Babe Ruth card." Trevor hesitated and looked away. He was afraid again.

"Yes, Trevor. What is it?"

"Please don't get mad . . . but . . . I . . . I . . . have something terrible to tell you." He had his great-grandpa's complete attention.

"I, . . . umm . . . I . . . lost the card. I didn't mean to do it," he said quickly. "But it's gone. I'm so sorry. I may have lost it . . . or it might have been stolen by some kids at school," he quickly blurted out. "I should've never taken it out of the house. I'm sorry. Please don't get mad." Trevor could feel the tears returning to his eyes.

Great-grandpa paused for a long moment. To Trevor, it seemed like forever.

"It's all right, Trev," he said reassuringly. "I'm not mad. It was just a piece of paper with a man's picture on it," he added.

"It was worth fifty thousand dollars," Trevor grieved.

"Anyone who'd spend fifty thousand dollars on a baseball card when there are so many starving and needy people in the world is a jerk."

Trevor looked at him, surprised that his great-grandpa used the word 'jerk.'

"Well . . . it's true," he stated. "Now, don't you worry about it, okay? I'm not mad. It'll turn up."

Trevor's mouth opened wide. He couldn't believe it. This was definitely *not* the reaction he expected. *I guess I don't know Great-grandpa that well after all*, Trevor thought. He couldn't believe that he would be forgiven so easily. "Well, okay. Thanks. I'm really sorry though, honest. You don't know what I've been through lately."

"I can imagine," his great-grandpa said. There was a special light in his eyes, a light that revealed his warm, loving and compassionate heart. Trevor saw in those eyes something he'd known all his life—love and friendship. "Trev, you know why I'm not mad?"

"No." Trevor answered. "But I sure am glad."

"Remember when I gave you the card on my birthday?"

"You bet."

"Remember what I told you?"

Jack Mitchell reminded Trevor about the true meaning of the card. The card was special not because of the man on it, but because it reminded him of how God intervened in his life in a miraculous way. The day he stole home off Babe Ruth marked the beginning of Trevor's great-grandfather's spiritual journey.

Babe Ruth was a great baseball player, but on and off the field, the Babe had dabbled in many of the sinful pleasures the world has to offer. If anyone needed the Lord's grace, it was definitely Babe. Trevor's great-grandfather did hear Babe Ruth give credit to the Giver of All Good

Things once after his "Called Shot"–a homerun that he called and hit after he pointed to the center field bleachers with his bat. After he hit it, he said, "The Good Lord must've been with me that day." Perhaps Babe Ruth really did know who blessed him with that great talent.

"Do you understand the card's meaning, son?" Great-grandpa asked.

"Yeah, I understand," Trevor said sincerely.

"Good. Then with or without the card, always remember the story. Baseball is a great game, but after all, it is just a game. I believe you know and love God with all your heart, and you will use your gifts to glorify Him in whatever you do. Just remember how faithful God is to us."

"You bet, Great-grandpa. I will," Trevor promised, kissing his favorite old-timer.

Then Trevor told Great-grandpa his whole story. He included how he had one more suspect to investigate–and how the principal was going to call soon with a special invitation. He told him how the kids at school didn't believe the story–and even more important, that the principal was going to ask him to bring the Babe Ruth card to the assembly . . . if he went.

"Well," Jack Mitchell said. "We'll just have to do something about that!"

"But what?" Trevor asked.

"I don't know. But we'll pray for wisdom."

"In all things, God works for the good of those who love him," Trevor added. He memorized that Scripture verse three weeks ago for Sunday school. It sure came in handy now.

"That's right," Great-grandpa said, smiling. "That's right."

CHAPTER TWELVE

Old Timer's Day

The Calvin Coolidge Elementary School gymnasium was filled with fourth through sixth-graders. Considering there were children with varying degrees of attention spans in the audience, they were well behaved as Jack Mitchell began his talk. In truth, they were mesmerized by the old man and the unbelievable story he related to them. Great-grandpa was wearing his old, woolen Detroit Tigers jersey, which looked older than he did, and a Tigers cap. The cap was new, a present from Trevor's father last Christmas.

Jack had two things in his favor on this day. First, most of the kids had never seen a one hundred year-old man. Second, it was only some of the kids in Trevor's sixth grade class who didn't believe the story. The rest either didn't have an opinion or didn't really care.

Trevor sat strategically in the front row, off to the left, where he could keep an eye on certain people. It was hard for Trevor to sit still. A secret operation was underway. He was excited, worried and anxious all at the same time. *I hope this plan works*, he thought.

Mr. Jenkins and all the teachers sat off to the side.

Everyone was focused on Trevor's great-grandpa as he told the amazing story they were all a bit familiar with.

"You should have seen the look on Babe Ruth's face," Mr. Mitchell concluded. "He looked like I spiked his gum with hot salsa."

The crowd laughed, especially Mr. Jenkins.

"And never before and never since had anyone stolen home off Babe Ruth. God was surely with me that day."

"What a crock."

It was said softly, but loud enough for everyone, even Great-grandpa to hear it. The comment caused some kids to laugh. Mr. Jenkins looked fiercely into the crowd to try to figure out who said it and give an unspoken message not to say another word. Trevor looked down, though. He recognized the voice.

Jack Mitchell appeared unaffected by the rude comment. "Now . . . your principal, Mr. Jenkins, asked me if I would bring the Babe Ruth card to show you guys . . . I know many of you haven't seen many things that old. Heck, I'm probably the oldest thing you've ever seen."

The kids and teachers laughed again.

"I've got one foot in the grave and another on a banana peel." There it was again–Great-grandpa's favorite line.

Great-grandpa looked at Trevor and nodded. "Operation Curveball," as they called it, was about to take place. "Where was I? Oh, yes . . . the card. How many of you are interested in seeing it?"

Almost all the children raised their hands. "All righty then. Well . . ."

Here we go. Trevor quickly looked into the audience and spotted his target. There were others he'd like to watch too, but only one person mattered right now.

"Well, here it is." With that said, his great-grandpa reached into the pocket of his navy blue slacks and pulled out a Babe Ruth rookie card in a plastic holder. Trevor's eyes were locked on Tom Murphy.

Gasps and words like "cool" and "neat" were heard from the crowd, mostly from boys and girls who loved collecting various sport cards; others were from kids who just liked seeing something so old. But Tom Murphy's reaction was . . . *nothing. Not even a blink. No double take? No look of shock? I don't believe it!*

Trevor's eyes grew wide, and his mouth dropped open. Operation Curveball didn't work. Tom Murphy looked at the card just like everyone else. *I guess he didn't take it. But who did then?* Trevor quickly looked at his great-grandpa. *What do we do now?* His great-grandpa understood from Trevor's eyes that the plan didn't work. He turned his attention back to the assembly.

"I want you to know that this card, even though it may be old and worth a lot of money, isn't as important as everyone thinks it is," Great-grandpa said.

Fact is, the card he held in his hand wasn't old at all. Trevor and his great-grandpa went to Charlie's Sports Collectibles and told him what happened. They wanted to see if anyone had tried to sell a 1915 Babe Ruth rookie card. No one had, but then it occurred to Great-grandpa that they needed something to show the kids at the assembly. That way no one would know that Trevor didn't have the card anymore. Operation Curveball was subsequently born. The card in his hand was a reprint that Charlie ordered and had overnighted to the Mitchell family. The shipping cost was significantly more than the two-dollar card.

"What's important is that you all know that anything

can happen in life." Great-grandpa paused and looked at Mr. Jenkins for a cue. Mr. Jenkins motioned for him to go on.

"All right then. Does anyone have any questions?"

He looked out over the crowd. So did Trevor.

"I do!" a voice proclaimed.

"What's your name son?" Great-grandpa asked.

"Frank Carbone."

Trevor looked down and shook his head. *Oh great.*

"How do you explain that there are no records of the game when you stole home?"

"I see you've read the article," Great-grandpa said. "Well, Frank, to be honest, I can't explain it. Only God knows. I don't really know what happened. I take it you don't believe me?"

Frank was on the spot. He never expected he'd be challenged, and he didn't want to be rude, but he was, after all, *Frank Carbone*, and Frank Carbone doesn't back down from anything. "Well, to be honest . . . No, I don't believe it. Babe Ruth was the greatest. If there were records to prove it . . ."

Jack Mitchell smiled at Frank. "Frank, you obviously know your baseball. Babe Ruth was great, but he was only a man, no different than you or me other than he was a great baseball player. You're a bright young man and not the first person to bring up the question about the records. All I can tell you is that's what happened. There can't be records for all of our accomplishments." Great-grandpa paused. Then he had an inspiration. "Which leads me to what I really wanted to share with you today.

"All of our accomplishments, like stealing home off Babe Ruth, or the stuff we own, our possessions, like this baseball card . . . they don't really matter at all."

The kids all looked at him curiously. They had been

taught the total opposite for years. Even Mr. Jenkins and the teachers looked at Great-grandpa curiously.

"What matters most is . . . well, look around you. Go ahead, look around."

All the children, parents and teachers looked to their left and right, not exactly sure of what they were supposed to be looking at.

"What you see here, your friends, teachers, your parents . . . they are what really matter. Believe me . . . it all goes by so fast. It seems like only yesterday when I was your age. When you're old like me, you'll think back to Coolidge School and remember your friends who you studied with, played with and dreamed with. I want you to think about it this way, and it's the last thing I'm going to say. There are only two things that matter in life, God and the people He created. They are the only two things that can last forever. Don't ever forget that and then you will have a rich, full life."

There was complete silence until a few of the teachers realized that he really wasn't going to say anything more. They started to clap, and soon the whole assembly hall was clapping. *I want to be just like you, Great-grandpa.* Trevor thought proudly. The fact that Operation Curveball flopped didn't matter anymore. Hearing the words spoken from a man like his Great-grandpa made quite an impression on anyone on the receiving end. No one would ever forget this assembly. Mr. Jenkins got up, shook Great-grandpa's hand and escorted him off the stage.

"Hey, Mitchell!" It was Tom Murphy and Frank Carbone.

The assembly was long over. The bell had rung. Everyone else was leaving to go home.

73

Oh boy. What do they want now? "Hey . . . listen. I don't want to hear anymore 'bout this lying stuff, okay . . ." Trevor started.

"We weren't going to," Tom said. Then he looked at Frank. "Actually . . . I think your great-grandpa's pretty cool," Tom said.

"You do?" Trevor was shocked.

"Yeah, and I was wondering if maybe you could get me his autograph . . . on a baseball?"

Frank looked at Tom as if he was crazy.

Trevor was taken aback by the question. Then he had an idea . . . he thought he'd investigate some more, just to be sure. "How'd you guys like that card?" Trevor asked.

"It's cool," Tom said. "I wish my dad or grandpa kept something like that from when they were kids."

Huh? They have no idea, Trevor thought.

"So . . . about the ball, could you?" Tom asked again.

"You want one, too?" Trevor asked Frank.

Frank paused. "No, that's all right, Mitchell. I still don't think it ever happened," Frank replied.

"Suit yourself. Maybe someday you'll learn how to have faith."

"Nice try, Mitchell. I don't think so."

Trevor turned his attention to Tom. "Tell you what, you supply the ball and I'll get you the autograph."

"Thanks," Tom replied.

Trevor looked at Frank who obviously felt awkward. Trevor stuck out his hand. "Listen, Frank, just because you don't believe my great-grandpa doesn't mean we can't be friends. What do ya say?"

Frank looked at Trevor's hand. Tom looked at Frank as if to say, "Shake it." "Well . . . I heard my dad say he's gonna try and draft you for our team next year, so since we may

74

be on the same team, I guess it's all right." He shook his hand quickly . . . and uncomfortably. It was clear that Frank wasn't used to making up with anyone.

Trevor was speechless. He hadn't really expected Frank to accept his offer.

"We'll see ya later," said Tom as he and Frank walked away.

"Yeah . . . see you later," Trevor said. The boys headed off, down the hall. Trevor then noticed Ginger walking out of her classroom. He waved and smiled at her. She smiled in return. *Good. She's not mad at me anymore.*

The card was still gone, but things were looking up for Trevor. He felt some sort of order returning to his life, and his posture and the way he walked reflected it.

Coming down the hallway toward him was Whitey. He was alone. He casually bent down to get a drink from the water fountain as Trevor approached. Then suddenly, he jolted upright as a stream of water launched toward the sky. His face was dripping wet. Somebody had jammed a piece of popsicle stick in the fountain, causing it to act like a high-pressure squirt gun.

"A little thirsty, Whitey?" Trevor said, laughing. "The water's supposed to go inside your mouth." It was the first joke from Trevor in days.

"Very funny," Whitey replied. "Did you do that?" he said, referring to the popsicle stick.

"No. *You* probably did it and forgot it was there," Trevor joked.

"What are you so happy about?"

"Oh, nothing. I'm just feeling good. God is good. Hey... how'd you like the assembly?"

"It was cool. Your great-grandpa's really old, man. He probably graduated with George Washington."

"Very funny," Trevor replied, sarcastically.

"You're lucky Carbone didn't give him a harder time."

"I gotta tell you something 'bout that card," Trevor said.

"Yeah . . . I must've missed something in the article. I didn't know he had two cards."

Trevor froze. "What do you mean?" he said with extreme curiosity.

"You have two cards," Whitey said matter-of-factly.

"What makes you think I have two?"

"Huh?" Whitey grunted, not understanding the questioning at all. "What do you mean?"

The look on Trevor's face got very serious, and Whitey realized something wasn't right.

"How do you know I didn't find mine? What makes you think there are two cards?"

"What are you talking about?" Whitey asked, realizing he had slipped up.

"Nobody knows there are two cards. Why do you think there are two?" Trevor said seriously.

"Well . . . uh . . ." Whitey fumbled for an answer.

Trevor's countenance suddenly changed. His thoughts were racing and so was his pulse. He snapped inside.

"It *was* you, wasn't it? You took my card! I can't believe it!"

"What are you talking about, Mitchell? I didn't take your stupid card," Whitey said, starting to hurry away.

"Then how do you know there are two cards? Nobody knows that except my family."

"I didn't take your stupid card, man! It was probably Murphy or someone else that was at your stupid fight. I wasn't there, remember?" Whitey said, trying to avoid Trevor as he blocked Whitey's path with his body.

76

"Then how do you know? Tell me!" Trevor was more serious now than he'd ever been in his whole life. He was in Whitey's face, practically in Whitey's shoes.

Whitey gave no response. Other kids began to notice and slowed down as they walked by. Some even stopped to watch.

"That card is worth a lot of money. It means a lot to my family! Whoever stole it could be arrested. I want the truth, Scott," Trevor demanded. "Did you take it? Tell me right now." There was a lump in Trevor's throat that felt like an apple. He started to shake. He could feel his anger building.

Whitey looked around at the kids who were staring at him. He then turned to Trevor. "No! I didn't take your card! Now get out of my face! You're such a loser, Mitchell! No wonder nobody likes you!" Whitey pushed Trevor aside and walked away.

His last statement was a lie. The other kids did like Trevor. They had no idea what was going on, but they knew it was serious. Ginger overheard most of what had just transpired.

"What's going on?" she asked.

"It's a long story," Trevor replied.

"Is this what you couldn't tell me about?"

"Yep," Trevor answered, and he just watched Whitey hurrying down the hall. Trevor had no idea what to do next. But he knew he was going to do something.

CHAPTER THIRTEEN
The Unexpected

The weekend came, and things were still out of the ordinary for the Mitchell family. The phone was ringing off the hook with people calling about the article. It was appearing in more papers across the country. They also received some disturbing crank calls from Babe Ruth fans who said Great-grandpa was a "nut." Other calls came saying Great-grandpa was a liar. Representatives from additional popular television shows called, too. CNN was still broadcasting the segment as well. It was a terrific story and mostly everyone loved it. They also loved Trevor's great-grandpa.

The family talked it over and decided it would be best if Great-grandpa didn't appear on TV anymore. They wanted the craziness to end.

A couple of "crazies," as Great-grandpa called them, phoned with offers to buy the card. Trevor's father simply told them the card was *not* for sale.

Trevor could not get Whitey out of his mind. He replayed their conversation over and over in his mind. He told his parents and great-grandpa about it, but they couldn't call Whitey's parents and accuse him. It just wouldn't be right. They all did the only thing that mattered most—pray.

Then, on Sunday afternoon, right after church, a telegram arrived at the Mitchell home. It was addressed to Jack Mitchell from a man named Tom McCullough who lived in Florida. Trevor's great-grandpa had never heard of him. Tom McCullough was one hundred and *eight* years old. The telegram read, "Saw your story on CNN. Glad to know you're still alive. Happy Birthday from someone eight years your senior, who was at the game. You certainly showed up Babe Ruth that day. I can still remember your great slide into home. It seems like yesterday! Best regards, Tom McCullough."

Tom McCullough had often wondered what happened to the young rookie who stole home that day. The rookie showed promise. He didn't know that Jack Mitchell only played two years in the majors for Detroit and then had to stop playing because of a bad knee.

Trevor's great-grandfather read the telegram and immediately had to sit down. His eyes became misty, and a big tear rolled down his wrinkled cheek. After all these years, here was his proof. More than that, it just felt good to be remembered.

"One hundred and eight years old. Well, I'll be. Thank you, Tom. Thank you very much," Trevor's great grandpa said softly to himself.

"What, Grandpa? Who's it from?" Trevor's mom asked.

Everyone gathered around Trevor's great-grandpa. He passed it to his mom first. She read it and became teary-eyed, too. She passed the message to her husband who

80

passed it to Kirsten who passed it to Trevor. Everyone was moved. Trevor finished reading the last line and looked up at everyone with a big smile. They all embraced. It was the family's finest moment. God had provided a special blessing for all of them!

Later that evening, Trevor's great-grandpa called information and got the number for Tom McCullough in Cocoa Beach, Florida. He called Tom, and the two of them spoke for nearly an hour. The main topic of conversation was, of course, baseball. Baseball has a special way of bridging communication gaps–even among people who have only just met.

No sooner had Trevor's great-grandpa hung up the phone when it rang again. It was another surprise. Trevor's mom answered the call. The news she heard was both good and bad.

The woman on the other end of the line was Mrs. Whiteman, Whitey's mom. About an hour ago, Whitey had confessed to her that he had stolen the baseball card. He felt terrible. He was still crying in his room. She felt terrible, too. Trevor's mom was thrilled and relieved to know that the card was found, but saddened that Whitey had actually stolen the card. She was a mom, too, and could understand how sad Whitey's mom must be right now.

"Thank you, Mrs. Whiteman. We're very pleased to know that you have Trevor's card. Do you want us to pick it up?" There was a long pause. "Are you sure you want to do it that way?" There was another pause. "All right . . . no . . . it's all right. Yes . . . I'll talk to you soon." Then she hung up.

She took a deep breath. "John! Grandpa! Kids! Everyone come in here for a minute, please!" she yelled into the next room.

She told everyone that Whitey had the card. On the day the card disappeared, Whitey was walking behind Trevor on the way home from school. He saw Trevor performing his good deed for Mrs. Younger and he saw the backpack. Whitey knew the card was inside so he took it when no one was looking.

Trevor was relieved to know that they were going to get the card back, but he felt angry and betrayed. He was hoping he hadn't taken it.

"How are we gonna get it back?" Kirsten asked.

"Well, I'm a little surprised by that part. Mrs. Whiteman is insisting that Scott give it back to Trevor at school tomorrow."

Trevor's eyes grew wide. "What! I don't even want to see him! Doesn't he know what he put me through?" *Good thing I didn't actually accuse any of those other guys of taking it.* Trevor felt terrible for even thinking such thoughts about the other boys.

"That's how she wants to do it," his mom stated.

"Think how Whitey is feeling right now," his father said, "knowing he has to face you. The good news is that we're getting the card back though, right Grandpa?"

"God is faithful, and he answers prayer," Trevor's great-grandpa said with a smile. "But that poor little boy . . ."

"We'll pray for him," Kirsten exclaimed.

Trevor was not quite as compassionate as the rest of his family. *How can they all forgive Whitey so easily after what I've been going through?*

CHAPTER FOURTEEN

Duty

Trevor's walk to school the next morning was long and hard. He was excited to get his card back, but he did not want to see Whitey. He was still really angry.

I can't believe he did this to me. He was my friend. Trevor couldn't understand what would make Whitey steal from him. He had always been nice to Whitey. He helped him with his homework, and when other kids wouldn't talk to him or hang out with him, Trevor always would. That's what a friend was to Trevor, someone who was always there—and who would *never* steal from you.

He's no friend of mine, and he NEVER will be again, Trevor thought, approaching the school grounds. *I'm just gonna take the card back and walk away.* Trevor thought about punching Whitey. He was certainly mad enough, but he knew that wouldn't solve anything.

Trevor walked onto school property, passed the swing set, and there he was. Whitey stood against the wall by the door to their wing. He was looking about as happy as

Trevor looked. Actually, he looked worse. Whitey was scared, and he knew what he did was terribly wrong.

Trevor walked up to him quickly. *Let's get this over with and be done with it.*

The two looked at each other awkwardly, not sure who should speak first.

"Can I have my card back . . . please?" Trevor took control.

"Yeah." Whitey reached into his backpack and handed it to him.

Trevor checked it thoroughly to make sure it was not harmed. It looked fine.

Trevor didn't say a word. He just looked at Whitey, shook his head, then headed for the door. The bell was about to ring, and kids were starting to gather and walk by.

"Wait!" It was Whitey.

Trevor turned around.

"What?" He looked Whitey in the eye.

"I want you to know . . . I'm sorry."

Trevor paused for a moment.

"Sorry? I don't believe you, Whiteman."

"Really, Trev. I'm really sorry I took it."

"Why'd you do it?" Trevor asked.

"I don't know why. I saw the backpack sitting there and something inside said, 'Take it.' I knew it was wrong, but I couldn't help myself. I felt terrible ever since. I didn't know how to get it back to you."

"How long were you gonna wait?"

"I don't know. I didn't know what to do. I don't have any good answers. I'm sorry."

Trevor looked into Whitey's eyes. What did he see? Whitey looked sincere. Trevor thought about asking

Whitey if he knew how much trouble he caused or if his mother had grounded him for life. Then it occurred to him how he felt when he had asked his great-grandpa and his parents to forgive him. He had lost the card, broken the rule and taken the card to school. No one had bombarded him with questions. No one had refused to forgive him.

Trevor realized he was wrong now. His anger melted, and he looked at Whitey kindly. "Okay. Apology accepted."

Whitey smiled with relief.

Forgiving isn't easy sometimes, but Trevor knew he had to forgive as he had been forgiven by his family. It was his duty. It was the right thing to do. He would have forgiven Whitey in his own heart later anyway, after he had time to process everything. He knew that.

"Thanks," Whitey said, breathing a sigh of relief.

"No problem," Trevor said. "It took a lot of guts to do what you just did."

"It wasn't easy."

"Not many things are easy. I'm learning that too." They smiled at one another.

Trevor held the card tightly in his hand. There was no way he was going to put Babe Ruth back in his knapsack. He would call his mom to come get it from him. *That's what I'll do.* Then he wondered if he and Whitey would ever be friends again. Somehow, he knew they would.

Trevor opened the door for Whitey, and the two boys went into the school building. Lessons, it seemed, weren't always learned from textbooks. The lessons that Trevor learned during the past few weeks–about faith, family, friendship and forgiveness–were lessons that he'd take with him and use every day for the rest of his life.

CHAPTER FIFTEEN
The Weaving

Trevor's great-grandpa passed away five years later. Trevor was sixteen. His great-grandpa was one hundred and five. The card was kept in a secret place in the Mitchell home. Only Trevor and his family knew where, and they looked at it often and remembered.

There were tears, of course, when Trevor's great-grandpa died, lots of them. Yet as sad as everyone felt, no one looked at death as if it was the end, because they knew Great-grandpa was now safe at home in heaven. Besides, everyone knows there must be baseball in heaven.

As he grew into manhood, Trevor became a man of character just like his great-grandpa–and he treasured his memories too.

With a little faith all things are possible, Trevor thought, remembering his great-grandpa as he brushed some of the dirt off his pants. He was standing on third base in Tiger Stadium, looking at the best pitcher in the major leagues– a rookie just like himself. He took another swipe at the dirt

87

on his pants as he thought about how much he loved and missed his great-grandpa. He knew he was watching from above and the thought of that made Trevor smile.

Then Trevor Mitchell took his lead and looked at the pitcher beginning his wind up. *This one's for you Great-grandpa. I love you.* He focused his eyes on home and ran.

Fact vs. Fiction

Here's an overview of the "fact vs. fiction" elements in *Safe at Home*. It's important that you know which portions are real and which portions are the author's imagination.

FACT

Babe Ruth's rookie card is really the 1915 Sporting News No. 151 card. When *Safe at Home* was written in 1997, the Babe Ruth rookie card was worth about $3,000 in near mint condition and the $50,000 value detailed in the story was fiction. However, over the years, the card has increased in value. In 2007, the card sold for $165,000 at an auction in mint condition.

FACT

Babe Ruth's rookie season was in 1914, when he began his career as a left-handed pitcher for the Boston Red Sox. Babe Ruth pitched 29 2/3 consecutive scoreless innings of World Series' play. He really did say, "The good Lord must have been with me that day," when he referred to his alleged "called shot" home run.

Mike McNally did play third base for the Boston Red Sox in 1915.

Christy Mathewson was nicknamed "The Christian Gentleman." Christy also promised his mom he would not pitch on Sunday.

FICTION

Jack Mitchell is a fictional character I created. I guess you could say he is my dream of what a very cool grandpa or great-grandpa would be like. Therefore, Trevor Mitchell and all the other characters are fictional as well. Trevor was named after my son.

The reference that there are four games in baseball history from 1911 to 1932 that no one has records of, including the Hall of Fame, is fiction.

FACT

There were at least two steals of home while Babe Ruth pitched in the major leagues. One was on May 16, 1916, when Ruth beat the Browns, 3-1. The only St. Louis score was on a double steal. The second was June 1, 1917, when Ruth lost to Cleveland, 3-0. One of the Indian tallies came on a double steal.

Source: *The Baseball Chronology*, by James Charlton, published by Macmillan in 1990.

I hope you had as much fun reading *Safe at Home* as I had writing it.

Robert Skead

BABE RUTH
P.—Boston Red Sox
151
REPRINT

The 1915 Sporting News Babe Ruth rookie card

(Photocopy the image above on card stock
and cut it out to make your own card.)